LENEY BIN, CHURCH GROVE
CROOKED ISLAND

ISLES OF EDEN

For Aperture

Harvey Lloyd

LIFE IN THE SOUTHERN FAMILY ISLANDS OF THE BAHAMAS
Columbus Quincentennial Edition

Text and Photographs by
HARVEY LLOYD

Photographs on pages 52–55 by Barry Benjamin

Benjamin Publishing, Co., Inc.   Akron, Ohio   © 1991

Harvey Lloyd text and photographs
© 1991 Harvey Lloyd

Barry Benjamin photographs

© 1991 Benjamin Publishing Company, Inc.

All rights reserved. The use of any part of this publication, reproduced, transmitted in any form or by any means, electronic, mechanical, photocopying, recording or otherwise, or stored in a retrieval system, without the prior consent of the publisher, is an infringement of copyright law and is forbidden.

Library of Congress Cataloging in Publication Data

Lloyd, Harvey.
  Isles of Eden : life in the southern family islands of the Bahamas / text and photographs by Harvey Lloyd. -- Columbus Quincentennial ed.
    p.   cm.
  ISBN 0-9629806-0-9: $65
  1. Bahamas--Description and travel--1981- 2. Bahamas--Description and travel--1981-   --Views. I. Title.
F1651.L58   1991   91-4971
972.96--dc20   CIP

Front & Back Cover: Detail of rusting shipwreck, San Salvador

Front End Papers: Aerial View— Osprey Cay, Exuma Chain

Back End Papers: Aerial View— Waters between Long Island and Exumas

Photos by Barry Benjamin

pages 52–55

Field Recording and Transcription by: Shirlee Price

Designed by: Modino Graphics
Maureen O'Brien and
Dean Papparlardo

Edited by: Caroline Baumann

Map by: Garnet Henderson

Printed in Japan

Foreword

By Rt. Hon. Sir Lynden Pindling, Prime Minister and Minister of Tourism of the Commonwealth of the Bahamas

The islands of the Bahamas have been known by many names over the centuries. The name the nation bears today, for example, was derived from *bajamar*, the Spanish term for "shallow seas". The Lucayans, the original Bahamians, left behind mellifluous place names such as "Mayaguana" and "Bimini", which remain as lasting memorials to their culture. It was on the "Guanahani" of the Lucayans (renamed San Salvador by the "Discoverer" himself) where east first met west, when Christopher Columbus made his first landfall in the New World in 1492.

I imagine most people who have travelled among the islands, especially those who have sailed the waters of our archipelago, have called our islands by names which convey something of the emotional impact which our islands can have on the imagination. To some, the Bahamas are the "Islands of Romance" and to others, the "Sailor's Paradise". I think, however, that *Isles of Eden* best captures the pristine beauty by which our islands are still distinguished, the very quality by which Columbus himself seemed most moved. Our islands seldom fail to stir the imagination and stimulate the soul. They have, clearly, done so for writer/photographer, Harvey Lloyd, and photographer/publisher, Barry Benjamin, who have travelled among our islands and their people for many years, writing of their experiences and capturing images of our life-style and environment on film. The results are found on the pages of this wonderful book.

As you read *Isles of Eden*, you will feel the love which Messrs. Lloyd and Benjamin have come to feel for our people and our country. I hope you will be moved by the experience to do as they did: look further, beyond the initial impression derived from a short vacation trip. Return and spend a longer time, travelling further afield. You, too, will be rewarded with an experience you will never forget; though you may not produce a marvellous, tangible documentation, like *Isles of Eden*, I am certain that a record, just as indelible, will "linger in the memory".

ACKNOWLEDGMENTS

My first thanks go to the welcoming people of the Family Islands of the Bahamas who with warm hospitality, patience, and love contributed their words and their images to these pages. This book is theirs.

I thank Stan and Barry Benjamin for supporting this project with enthusiasm. I would also like to thank: Jeanne and Becky Benjamin for their help and ideas; the government of the Bahamas and the local government of Great Exuma for their kind cooperation; Charles Pflueger, manager of the Club Peace and Plenty, our base in George Town, Great Exuma, and his always cheerful and efficient staff; pilot Clifford Dean who first introduced me to the wonders of the waters round Great Exuma and the Exuma Chain; Maureen O'Brien and Dean Pappalardo of Modino Graphics; David Hansen for his publishing know-how; Mike Remer for wise counsel; Caroline Baumann for editing the text.

A debt of gratitude to my friend and companion Shirlee Price, who not only recorded and transcribed the many voices of the Family Islanders, but provided invaluable guidance and advice at every stage of this book. Thanks to my son Andrei Lloyd for his suggestions and unfailing encouragement.

These photographs appear on the following pages: T.M. Williams, Colonel Hill, Crooked Island, 36; Estella Chisolm [93 years old], Colonel Hill, Crooked Island, 37; Edwin L. Butler, George L. Lightfoot, Reckley Hill, San Salvador, 80; Caroline & Edward Ferguson, Major Cay, Crooked Island, 81; Arimina and Uznor Musgrove, Moss Town, Great Exuma, 86–87.

ATLANTIC OCEAN

ELEUTHERA

CAT ISLAND

SAN SALVADOR
UNITED ESTATES
LONG BAY

FARMER'S CAY
BARRATERRE
ROLLEVILLE

RUM CAY

GREAT EXUMA

GEORGE TOWN
STELLA MARIS
WILLIAMS TOWN
DEADMAN'S CAY

LITTLE EXUMA

LONG ISLAND

PITTSTOWN LANDING
FAIRFIELD

CROOKED ISLAND

ACKLINS ISLAND

BAHAMAS

GRAND BAHAMA
ABACO
ELEUTHERA
NEW PROVIDENCE
NASSAU
ANDROS

CAT ISLAND
SAN SALVADOR
RUM CAY
GREAT EXUMA
LONG ISLAND
CROOCKED ISLAND
ACKLINS

GARNET

INTRODUCTION

When Columbus had his vision Grand
Of the world beyond the sea
His faith and dauntless spirit
Soared when the
sovereign heard his plea
Now the old and the new world both
Rejoice and the echoes sound afar
Of the lovely isle
The New World's light
Glorious San Salvador.

San Salvador, I hear you calling
across the sea to me.
The blessed isle, the brightest gem
in the crown of destiny.
San Salvador I hear you call
Thrice blessed isles, San Salvador

During our stay in San Salvador, ninety-seven-year-old Ethelyn Wring sang the Columbus song and other melodies from her childhood in a rich, but faintly cracked voice. Surrounded by her children and grandchildren in her tiny wooden home, she gazed at us with an expression filled with goodness and joy. A tremendous sense of caring and tenderness pervaded this family gathering—a feeling we would encounter again and again during visits with the people of the Southern Family Islands of the Bahamas.

The Spanish were the first Europeans to explore these Southern Bahamian islands. Columbus is said to have made his first landing in the New World on San Salvador. A large white cross and a row of flags mark his arrival spot on the beach. Columbus also visited Long Island and Crooked Island, areas documented in this book. The Spaniards called the sea *bajamar*, or shallow sea. The name Bahama Islands literally means the islands of the shallow sea.

The people, especially the older natives and the long time settlers retain a simplicity and an openness that reflect their bond with nature and with the sea that surrounds their narrow, crooked islands and cays (pronounced keys). Caught up in a world that is troubled with the dangers of encroachment on the natural environment and overly burdened by the concerns of civilization, we can benefit greatly from the gentle wisdom and ever-present caring for other human beings found on these *Isles of Eden*.

During my many travels over our water planet, I have never once encountered seas to compare with the dazzling green and turquoise waters of the Southern Bahamian Islands. From the air, long crooked islands and green cays are visible, scattered amidst a riotous profusion of emerald dyed waters, resembling the paintings of the abstract expressionist school.

The tides that swirl around the shallow sea bottom and the white sand banks, cays, and purple-blue cuts sculpt the sand and cause these abstract color patterns. Like a desert mirage, this vision comes and goes with the changing light. The imaginative mind 'sees' shapes from dreams and nightmares, creatures from the deep, wild birds, fish, animals. The waters encourage limitless fantasy.

Isles of Eden celebrates the sea and the people who owe allegiance to the sea. The sea is the arbiter of the lives of all who reside on these Southern islands of the Bahamas, moderating the temperature and providing a bounty of food. Coral reefs, the underpinnings of these painted waters, keep the great banks of shallow seas in place. Small airplanes that fly from island to island and from cay to cay, private yachts and ferry boats that cruise the islands acquaint the visitors with the myriad cays and the narrow, crooked islands. The trade winds blow incessantly and the hurricanes in their season. The low lying islands give little shelter. Fortunately, the sea is compassionate, rarely sending great storms. Those that do come, such as the ravaging hurricanes of 1908 and 1926, are well remembered by the older folk. Mrs. Violet Bain of Rum Cay recalls:

"I was still a teenager and this September day of 1926 was the worst for Rum Cay. Father was on a boat to San Salvador—we never saw him again. And for the salt (industry) it was all over. The dam broke and the ocean water filled in and destroyed all the pans. Everything else went down too."

Island Expedition, 1988

For the ships that sailed there in the early days, the shallow seas, sand banks, and sharp coral reefs created a hazardous obstacle course. Encrusted with reefs too numerous to chart, the seas took their pitiless toll of sailing ships. Many of those spared by the sea fell prey to the pirates of the Spanish Main, and then to the wreckers who brutishly picked over the bones of their ships. Today, lighthouses, radar, and more accurate charts make these always perilous sea lanes safer.

The southern chain of cays and islands comprising the Exumas, San Salvador, Long Island, Rum Cay, Cat Island, and Crooked Island stretches several hundred miles southeasterly from Nassau almost to Haiti. Beneath the sea, a mountain-like land mass divides and redivides to form twenty or more flat topped summits. Peaks and ridges break the water. These "mountain tops" make up the islands of the Bahamas. The gorges separating the summits are the deep water cuts, or passages.

The seas, though shallow, reveal little of the fantastic underwater geography. Like a neon-lit palette of iridescent greens and blues and turquoises, the waters glow in the midday sunshine. The white sand banks resemble scimitars, cutting knife-edge arabesques through the waters. White clouds hover over a purplish, hazy, and nearly invisible horizon. Islands and cays abound; the two words are often interchanged. In essence, a small island is a cay. A large cay, such as Rum Cay, is an island. The decision to name a given piece of land either as an island or as a cay is arbitrary, and purely up to the islanders' fancy, as are the names themselves.

"Deadman's Cay, that's a hell of a name. Tell a foreigner you're going to Deadman's Cay airport . . . that doesn't sound like a nice place to come."

Delbert Cartwright

One islander described the land masses spotting the sea as mainly rock and stones. And so they are, and soil is scant, although windblown sand called white soil accumulates to considerable depth in places. On these southern islands and cays, the vegetation is of the scrub variety, with few trees. Windward coasts are blustery, scrubbed by the prevailing winds and the action of the breaking waves. To the leeward, calm prevails and the water is still and transparent, glittering in the sunlight. Breezes are gentle. Rooted in the sea bed, dark green mangrove flourishes. Early sailors knew of the mangrove's liking for sheltered waters and sought safety there from approaching storms.

THE ISLANDERS

A gentle and kindly way of life persists on these narrow islands and tiny cays. Among the islands of the shallow sea, the sea is a benevolent master and provider. No heavy industry exists. The air is fragrant with the fresh winds from the sea and the sweet perfume of pineapples, cassava, and cantaloupes. Farming and fishing are a way of life. Recalling quieter days, the old folk long to keep their ways. They enjoy the deep-felt intertwining of their peaceful lives with the sea. People smile and wave, an artless art long gone from our own busy and uncaring urban civilizations. Ask for someone and a townsman will tell you whether they are at home, off the island, or exactly where they might be found on the island. Neatly attired in suits and ties and white dresses, the people gather on Sunday in the white churches. "Won't you come in?" they say, beckoning from the pews.

VISITING

At the north end of Great Exuma is the town of Anna's Track or Arne's Tractor or just *Annastrack*, depending on who you ask. We cross two short causeways that link Anna's Track and the larger town of Barraterre to the main island. At the end of the short dirt road in Anna's Track, Rosalee Wright farms sapodilla, bananas, tomatoes and peas. Across the road, Georgia Wright, who lives in a tiny old house, says she will only welcome us after we ask Rosalee's permission.

"Ah'm the boss," says Rosalee.

Rosalee lives alone in a big house. "My parents died, and my children moved away."

"Now you come down," she shouts at Georgia.

Reassured and allowing her friendliness to show, Georgia smiles at us. She is very old. Willie Wright hobbles out of the house after her. Willie had been a sturdy fisherman, but now his tall body is bent with 'ailments'. They stand together for the photograph. "God bless you," she says, "You won't be strangers when you come again."

(We did come back the next year. Georgia, Willie and Rosalee were nowhere to be found. In a nearby town, they informed us that Willie had died.)

At Barraterre, the local schoolmaster hacks a hole in a coconut with a machete and gives us fresh coconut milk. "You must photograph the children," he says.

He lines up the primary school children in front of the yellow schoolhouse. They are orderly and smile, not wild and out of control as is often the case. At the Fisherman's Inn, proprietor Norman Lloyd welcomes us. "I saw you all at breakfast at the Peace & Plenty in George Town," he says. In response to our question why he stays in so small and quiet a town of perhaps three hundred inhabitants, he replies, "Nassau, I like it to go, not to live. Where you're born you feel more relaxed." He grins. "Before the causeways, you had to come here by boat. We had a saying 'We bring you here by boat when you're ready. You don't leave when you're ready, you leave when we're ready.'"

He explains how the young people go to Nassau for work and for attractions not available on the tranquil, secluded islands. He thinks that the new airport may bring more work, and encourage some of the people to return. Norman has his own work to do. "Your name's Lloyd too," he says, "Come back again, cousin."

We buy a beer for the man who showed us the way to Fisherman's Inn. He does not feel up to going to work this morning. He asks for a few dollars. I reach into my wallet.

"Not here. Outside where they can't see me."

We drive off. A few miles down the road I see a woman in a bright red dress perched on the treads of a big yellow bulldozer, on the shady side. She is plaiting straw for baskets and revels in having her picture taken.

What is found in these islands of the shallow sea is unheard of in the big cities. Doors are never locked. If in need of groceries, one may buy or take them from the many 'stores' that occupy a section of many of the houses. A storekeeper explains: "I know everybody here, and everybody's grandchildren. I don't need to record anything. They know what they owe me they'll come and pay at the end of the month!"

Island Expedition, 1988

A warm-hearted and loving people. Progress is on the way. Perhaps it will come slowly. Farming and fishing. I remember Georgia Wright's words. "You won't be strangers when you come again."

THE ATLANTIC WATERS

The great banks of shallow waters resemble the vast desert landscapes of the southwestern United States in the way that they shimmer and glisten varied hues in the ever-changing light.

The painted desert of the sea reveals riotous shades of blues, emerald greens and turquoise. The brilliant sheen often colors the low hanging, billowy white clouds a pale green. Fantastic cloud castles march in ranks across the azure skies and modulate the light. The vast scalloped banks, the white and sinuous sand bars and the coral underpinnings of the sea combine to create a panorama of dazzling light sculptures.

At night, all is quiet except for the lapping of the sea and the sound of the surf on the windward shores. To a visitor from the city, the eternal racket is strangely gone. The air is clear. The wheel of the Milky Way turns overhead and the black velvet sky glitters with stars.

UNDER THE SEA — THE CORAL REEFS

The sand shifts constantly, scrubbed by the strong currents, and forming new sculpted patterns under the crystal waters. The queen conch, with its rosy pink shell, feeds and lives among the sea grasses that grow in sheltered locations. Sponges are widely distributed, though scarcer now than in the past.

The simple coral polyp is the architect of these banks, but the work is slow. The polyp likes a water temperature of around seventy degrees, and will not build reefs on ocean bottom much below eighty feet in depth. To build a reef twenty feet high requires thousands of years.

Varied underwater life inhabits the reef during its developing stages. Twig-like, pink gorgonians, straw-colored sea feathers and lacy, yellow and purple sea fans undulate below the clear green waters. Dark purple sponges, black, spiny sea urchins and yellow and brown sea-stars add to the gardens. Coral dominates and each coral colony boasts its own distinctive hue. The coral structures on the interior of the banks are 'shoals' or 'coral heads'. Dense, ever-transforming, and impossible to chart, they are a menace to ships.

To the windward, on the edge of the banks that lie between the islands and the ocean, the coral erects 'fringe reefs'. Although the coral appears delicate and fragile, it withstands the hurricanes and is strong enough to crush the steel plates on ships' bottoms.

The spiny lobster, a delicious staple of island food, lives under rocky shelves and in hidden crevices. The Bahamian fishermen, familiar with the innumerable variety of underwater life, fish just above these reefs, where grunts, yellow tails, porgies, snappers, angelfish, parrot fish, turbots, margate fish, groupers and rockfish swim.

THE SHALLOW SEA, AN EPILOGUE

On Sampson Cay, thirty miles or so north of Great Exuma, a young-looking woman with silvery-blonde hair explains that she had first come to the waters around Sampson Cay five years back to give birth.

"I gave birth under water. These were the clearest, purest waters I could find."

"How did you do it?"

"I squatted down. He came out and it was wonderful to watch him swim like a fish. You see I had heard that the Maoris of New Zealand gave birth that way, and I wanted to do the same." She laughed. "You see I met a Maori after that, and he told me that the truth was that only the gods in their legends gave birth that way."

I spent three days flying with Clifford Dean, who owns a big Piper Cherokee airplane and flies cargo in and out of George Town, Great Exuma. I sat in the cargo hold, with the door off, looking backward. We flew over the chain of cays towards Nassau, one hundred miles from George Town. I think now of the so-called 'rapture of the deep', experienced by divers who remain underwater for excessively long periods. I was drunk with the sight of the waters. Primitive feelings about the sea, the mother of all life on earth, welled inside of me. I wrote a long poem.

Excerpt from "The Rape of Eden":

Now Clifford,
 pilot, gentle necromancer,
 land your Piper Cherokee.
 Leave us once more here at
 the dusty airport.
Our dreams remain.

. . . While yet I am away
I will remember these flights
 with you,
  and on another day return
  that we may again
  begin our sacred aerial dance,
   our ritual,
   and o'er this vast
   paint pot,
    these emerald seas,
    this tract of shallow ocean,
    we may share with you,
    the golden hours when the
     sun's rays
    fall like shooting stars
    upon the cracked mirror of
    this shining sea.

We'll meet again,
 medicine man of the Cherokee.
 Once more, I'll shout,
 "Yonder, yonder, to the
 horizon."

"Ah yes, I tell you, I spent some good days in my life, home, and after I got married. I had no trouble. No kind of difficult rough time, or anything. So I am still here until now, but I'm looking to see my Lord coming for me. I don't know what time, but I'm getting ready for action, because I live here alone.

"Yes, my dear, I'm right here in the hands of the almighty God and I make myself content. I ain't worried about nothing. I have me son and me daughter. She is, I expect to take a trip to Nassau. Yes, sometime this end of May. I want to go there. I want to see the doctor anyhow. I'm not looking for no come back to what I was before because I know I'm far gone. But I just want to let me know how he finds me. I'm going by the mail, by the boat.

"I right here in the hands of Mercy. I only looking up to my Lord now. The Lord's still watching over you and me. That's right. I do hope we meet here again but if we don't the Lord has prepared a place for all of us to meet."

HATTIE MOXEY [98 YEARS OLD]
FARMER'S CAY

GLORIA PATIENCE, "THE SHARK LADY" "All these little houses that you see knocking around today with no roofs, no windows, no doors they were truly little Bahamian houses built back some of them in the early 1800's. The wall is made, what they do to get the lime they go and they get conch shells, they get sandstone rock and they get coral from the sea. They build what they call a lime kiln, it's built round and they put a layer of conch shells, they put a layer of hard wood—log wood or button wood—a layer of conch shells or coral. It's built until it's a pyramid. Then they take and light it all around and that will burn for weeks and they never touch it. They just let it stay there until a heavy rain comes and blow it."

"It's on Hog Cay, it came from Africa, that's a bongo tree. It's a very huge tree and it has a flower similar to the shaving brush tree flower. And in the 1926 hurricane on July 24th, 1926, she was toppled over but then she grew up again. And she's still there and it's the only one here in the Bahamas. The old man that told us about it was a true African, old Thomas Dorsett. He was my father's herder on Hog Cay. And he was sold when he was eleven years old from a ship that came here from Africa. And he worked on Hog Cay as a young man. When we went to Hog Cay he was an old man. That was in 1920 and he told us about the bongo tree.

"In years gone by all roads were kept clean. The island has changed a lot. I do hope that there won't be many more changes, because we want it as it is."

FOREST, GREAT EXUMA

ETHELYN WRING, JUVA MARCHE, SUSILEE
ANDERSON, DESERINE FORBES
UNITED ESTATES, SAN SALVADOR

San Salvador, I hear you calling
across the sea to me.
The blessed isle, the brightest gem
in the crown of destiny.
San Salvador I hear you call
Thrice blessed isles, San Salvador

Christopher Columbus whose name
And fame still shine
Bright on the page of history
As in the days of old.
Out on the Spanish ships they sailed
Made jokes and toasts and rhymes
Gallant sailor boys we are
That ship so safe and bold.

Here's a cheer for old San Salvador
The land be there by nature
Where scores of bidding beach and lakes
A pleasure surely makes.

When slavery was abolished
and the bell of freedom ring
I hear the children singing round
singing round for joy
Glory, glory hallelujah,
we are all now set gone free
Glory, glory hallelujah,
we are all now set gone free.

Gone the sunlight of her day,
Gone to yonder golden shore
Clasp her hand upon her breast
While we softly . . .
Gone the sunlight of her day
Little sister gone to sleep.

When I was single
Married was I craved
Now I am married, Lord,
And trouble all the time
Lord, I wish I was a single girl again.

I have no hat on my head
No shoe on my foot
My husband he's a drunkard,
Lord, I wish I was dead,
Lord, I wish I was a single girl again.

I took me in some wash
And made a dollar or two
My husband slipped round and stole it
Lord, I don't know what I'll do
Lord, I wish I was a single girl again.

Two little children lying in the bed
Both are damp and hungry
Lord, they covered up the head,
Lord, I wish I was a single girl again.

I have no shoe on my feet
No hat on my head
My husband he is a drunkard
Lord, I wish I was dead
Lord, I wish I was a single girl again.
Lord, I wish I was a single girl again.

"Some of the slave masters they was nice and kind, and some of them unkind. And this master, this day took the poor slave who leaning on his knee and praying, he say, 'What are you doing?' The poor man say, 'I'm praying to God to send rain for the grass to grow, for my master to eat grass, for my master's creatures to eat grass.' He said, 'If it don't have rain in the morning, a hundred lashes on your back.' And he prayed, prayed that night, and the next morning, it was floods of rain; he said, 'Thank God.'

"It's so much to talk about slavery. When slavery was abolished, there was an old lady and she say, 'Pull down the flag of slavery and hoist up the flag of freedom. Pull down the flag of slavery, they sing and dance. Oh they was so glad'.

"And they were so glad, that they sing, they sing and dance...Well, then, when I was a child I used to go to school, and sometimes we have very kind school master. And sometimes no. And when anyone that girls or boys are sick in school or dead, we have a little service for them, you know. One of them was sick, and this song, let me see if I can remember. I'm trying to remember that song, and teacher says 'Be silent, close hands, close eyes.' And we did it. 'Bow heads.' And we'd bow our heads.

"Oh yes, when I was growing up, we was a lot of young people together, you know. Summer time, we get dressed and we walk along the beach. Next time we get dressed, we go to another settlement, and when we get to the other settlement they have a dancing place, you know, big place. And we have a nice dance for the ladies and gentlemen.

DELBERT CARTWRIGHT "During the days of piracy these islands was overrun with pirates. They had Sir Henry Morgan and his fleet. They anchored down by Andros Island, because they have a bluff down there named after him and they had swans all in them.

"The outstanding one among them is Blackbeard. They have a tower in Nassau named after Blackbeard. And in George Town, in New Found Harbour out here and off Boris Harbour out here there was an English pirate by the name of Yellow Jacket. They called him Yellow Jacket. And he and his fleet anchored out here.

"Then the Ragged Island chain, chain of cays that runs down to Ragged Island they have another English pirate and they have a cay down there named after him called Darville's Cay because during a heavy hurricane he got shipwrecked there. And they took the long boat and they came up on the southern part of the island and him and his crew, they settled down there.

"Deadman's Cay, that's a hell of a name, doesn't sound like a nice place to come, but the first early settler who came there, he didn't settle on the mainland, he settled on one of the small islands off the mainland and he found a dead Indian there and he called it Deadman's Cay and the name stuck. When the Spaniards came they started to catch these Indians who hid all through caves on the island and on the off cays and a lot of them died from want and they was killed out and sold.

"I don't know of any great battles fought but I know there was some inner struggles between the Spaniards and the French and the English. And the French people moved into The Bight, too, but they lived on the hill top. And there was a run in between them and the Spaniards, but eventually there came a tidal wave and swept all the Spaniards away because their homes was down around the flats by the seashore and that was a little rich town there.

"These early settlers with these big plantations they had a few hundred slaves each one of them so when they was freed, they just gave them a certain portion of land and gave them the master's title and that why you see white Turnquests and black Turnquests and white Cartwrights and black Cartwrights. That's where it come in, and then you got some of these white people who took up with the colored people who came here, some settlements there's not any white people left at all—yellow and brown and red and green and blue and purple.

"When you have prosperity that can come, and you have too much prosperity, well, you know, everything follows that. In comes the gangsters and the murderers and the gamblers and so on the like. Then the peace and calm of the place is destroyed, And so we would want some prosperity, not no great amount of it.

"If you used to living a quiet life and close to nature, it teaches you a lot, and you have time to think and you have time to study.

"We leave our doors open, we go over there and you could stay for a week or ever so long. But I tell you locks only made for honest people anyhow. If a thief needs to come in, I don't care what you put onto it, he'll get into it. In Nassau they got a lot of these fancy jail houses, I call them, because they got couple of dogs and burglar bars and each door got about two chain locks and five other locks onto it. It take you half a night to lock up before you can get to bed. I don't think that's a nice way to live."

GARNET W. KNOWLS
ALLIGATOR BAY
SIMMS, LONG ISLAND

"And we have Gamalamie, which I have growing here, and strongback; a lot of men that lose love life and they want to make love again, so you boil the Gamalamie and the strongback and drink a couple of gallons of that and that straightens you right out you make love like mad. They're still used. Oh yes they do. Most of the jobs you go on where these people are working, you'll see a little pot on a fire, and they're brewing, they're making up a brew. And that's what it's for, for making love like that and never running out. That's for sure. This is authentic.

MARGARET "MAGGIE" NIXON
FARMER'S CAY

Then we had manila which was called sisal. They would cut the sisal, put it in the water and let it deteriorate and then take it out and clean it all off and then you had the beautiful white fiber. And that was bailed and shipped. Yes, they made manila rope." GLORIA PATIENCE

Willimena works at the Pittstown Landing Inn on the northwest tip of Crooked Island. Sassy, good-natured and exuberantly cheerful, Willimena is reputed to serve the best food on the island at her tiny restaurant in Land Rail. We ride from the inn to the nearby town of Land Rail in Willimena's old pickup truck. In the tiny town we meet a woman carrying a machete. She is pleased to have her picture taken in front of an old church. First, she puts down her machete.

We go to Colonel Hill. A ninety-three-year-old friend of Willimena's comes out of her house to have her picture taken. At the town of Timber Hill, we photograph an old man seated in front of his house on a small hill. He has forty acres, but he is too old to farm. On the way out of Cabbage Hill, Willimena drops two tires off for repair. The fixed tires are waiting, unguarded, on the roadside when we return several hours later.

The old folks have manners. And good manners, we were told on Great Exuma, will get you anywhere. Manners, character, they are the same. On this island, virtually untouched by contemporary civilization, all of the people have manners. They stand up straight and tall to have their pictures taken. What you see is what you get. They know exactly who they are and they don't pretend, act shy or embarrassed or pose. These people look you square in the eye.

We drive up a hill to the Southland Grocery and Variety Store in the town of Major Cay. The proprietors, Caroline and Edward Ferguson, stand straight and proud under their big store sign for their photograph. Holding hands, they glare at the camera a look that says "This is us." Married for fifty years, Caroline and Edward resemble a pair of entwined sturdy oaks.

The Crooked Islanders are honest, hard working folk. They possess little in the way of material goods. Their character and their dignity are gold. Everyone has pride. They make the most of what they have. They take care of each other. This kind of character is rare these days.

CURTAS A. MOSS
TIMBER HILL, CROOKED ISLAND

The Shark Lady's family came from Boston. They went down to Key West, Florida to start a cigar factory. Charles Trelawny Fitzgerald, was sent over in charge of St. John's Church in Nassau, "It's still standing," she says. He came to the Exumas and fell in love with Little Exuma, so he bought almost all of the island.

"My first husband was from Seattle, Washington and he went around the world in his yacht. I met him here and got married. We got as far as Panama and some of the crew got homesick. We turned around and we went to Nassau to live. I lived there for thirty-five years. My husband died and I met George, and we've been married now for thirty-two years. I have nine children, and about twenty-six grandchildren, and about eighteen great-grand.

"When I moved here—you need occupational therapy here—I went fishing. I started the fishing industry here in Exuma because when I came here in '69 there was no fishing. I used to go out in a boat and catch two or three hundred pounds of fish and take them in to Peace & Plenty and the Out Island Inn and sell it all, and I did that every day, and then I started my shark fishing at the same time, and that became a great thing.

"I make pendants from the large teeth, earrings from the small teeth, and necklaces from the spine. I used to go out every day except Sunday. The number of sharks I've caught up until now would be about twenty-three hundred. I don't catch the sharks as a sport. It's caught because I use them. Nothing goes back into the sea. When I am through with the shark, if I don't give the meat away, if it's too big, the rest of it is cut up, taken about three miles from here and buried for fertilizer, so it's not wasted.

In a husky, soprano voice and with a twinkle in her eye, Gloria says, "I used to sail other people's boats for them, and then I decided to get my own boat, The Barefoot Gal. And when I got her, I decided that it would be an all-girl topless crew. So I sailed for eight years with an all-girl topless crew.

"When I first suggested it, people said, 'Oh, you can't go out there and sail with topless girls—that's against the law.' I said, "Listen, that's God's water out there, and I can do as I bloody well feel like on it. You can't do a thing about it. Nobody owns the sea, that's international law. I won my first cup in the 1970's and I have a picture of the Prime Minister presenting me with that."

"I catch hammerheads, tigers, makos, black tips, white tips, lemons, and, umm, any shark that takes my line. It's a shame, I don't have any of the necklaces left, but I do string them with pearls . . . from the same store that the queen's dressmaker gets his pearls to trim her dresses with.

"The shark habits . . . I will say this much—that the shark is the most unpredictable creature in the sea I've seen. I do not suggest swimming at night because the shark cannot see very good. Most anything he hits, he will bite. And that's the way a lot of people get hurt, swimming in murky water where they can't see the shark coming. The shark hits something, so he just takes a piece out."

GLORIA PATIENCE, "THE SHARK LADY"
THE FERRY, LITTLE EXUMA

GENEVA AND BERLIE BURROWS
AND GRANDSON RICKY
MANGROVE BUSH, LONG ISLAND

ST. MARY'S CHURCH
BUILT CA. 1500 LONG ISLAND

VIRGINIA MUSGROVE, ESTHERMAE BODIE
HERMITAGE, GREAT EXUMA

DEACON GEORGE JONES, ZION BAPTIST CHURCH, FAIR FIELD, CROOKED ISLAND "And the church, I remember there was a time you couldn't get a seat in this church. You have to stand outside there, people used to stand outside, fill right up. And we had plenty people here; plenty pastors, officers and members in this church. But now it's down to only . . . we're here. It be holding on until the Lord should call us, whether by death or a second coming. But we're holding on. But right now, as it is, the church is so big. See they made the church, there were so many people they made the church with two roofs, and it's hard for us to keep up now. Pretty hard. Hard on us. Cause the members are small and then the work have to be done keep this building in order to have a church to come in. So we are fighting our best and by God of mercy we going to, we are going to be in the God business.

"I believe in striving. You see my father didn't have the opportunity to do for me as I do for them. Opportunity is around. You see as the situation when I was growing up there wasn't no radio. I have the opportunity. Opportunity you must pass it on. It's passed on from generation to generation. You write a book of it, history recorded in books. From brains to book. History goes from brains to book. Where there is no brains there is no book. Goes from nature into paper. I am a walking book. I'm handing down by generation to my grandchildren."

EMILY MOSS, ZION BAPTIST CHURCH
FAIR FIELD, CROOKED ISLAND

JOHN MCKIE, THOMPSON BAY, LONG ISLAND "What has living on this island meant to me? It's meant living, being alive. I felt like I'd come home. And that's just the way I felt—it was just like I'd come home.

"And you'd see a line of donkeys, maybe fifty, seventy-five donkeys tethered one to the next coming over the hills with two woven pantaliers, one on each side, these big baskets that you could almost sit in, full of pines, coming from the fields. And one man would be leading them from his horse, another man would be bringing up the stern. And over the hills, down to the beach, there would be the big anchored-out vessels and the long boats. They'd pile the pines in them, make a payment, and they'd row them out to the ships.

REUBEN BODIE, H. MUSGROVE, ALEXANDER BODIE
ST. PAUL'S BAPTIST CHURCH, GREAT EXUMA

"One thing about Long Islanders, they tend really to seem to seek to retain ties with their home island. They come back again and again and again. And a lot of them, their favorite dream is to come home and live here and they're doing it."

LAURA GIBSON, GLADYS SEARS [PASTOR], HILTON PINDER
CHURCH OF GOD, THE FERRY, LITTLE EXUMA

Hilton Pinder's voice rattled the windows in the Church of God, located a few hundred yards from the Shark Lady's house in the town of The Ferry. A powerfully built black man of medium height with a wide grin and sparkling eyes, Hilton Pinder preaches for the Church of God and says that he lives by the word of Jesus. In between trips around the islands to deliver The Word, Hilton works as a stone mason. "I tell the young people that they have to give a fair, honest day's work," he says. "I'm happy most of the the time, though sometimes I get troubled. I think of the Lord and it helps me to feel good.

"I have an urge to tell people what I feel of the Lord. I tell the young people how the Lord saved me and how they can be saved too. I go traveling out to various churches preaching the word of God. I preach in the streets a lot of times, too.

"I was preaching about the foolish man and the wise man. The wise man build his house on the rock and the foolish man build it on the sand. And on the sand it cannot stand, and the wind and the wave and the rain come down and it couldn't stand so it falls. But the man who build on the rock it stand, the house on the rock stand. The rock is Jesus. The wise man is the man who is going to accept the Lord, knowing that Jesus is the shelter. He'll shelter us. He'll preserve us."

Waving his arms as he speaks, Hilton clenches his big workman's hands to make his points. "We got to call on the Lord. Sometimes we get fearful and look around and see what's happening, like Peter when he walk on the water with Jesus, and as long as he keeps his eyes on the Lord he can walk on the water, but the moment he takes his eyes and look on the waves, then he falls.

There is little sign of progress in the town of The Ferry. The Church of God is a tiny white church on the narrow, main road. Gladys Sears is the pastor, a post she earned by accident when her aunt, the first pastor, was killed by an automobile in Nassau. When Bishop Johnson asked Gladys to take over, she happily accepted, eager to help people and to share the word of God. "People live in holiness. You've been born again in the spirit of the Lord, Jesus Christ. You have to feed the flock, give them the word of God from the Bible."

Laura Gibson, who lives in a pink house across from the Church of God, came to hear Hilton preach. At seventy-nine years old, Gladys says that growing up in The Ferry was hard, always working at the farm after school and there was seldom much food.

Laura says that the young people do not listen to the word of God. "People are doing things that they should not do. The devil get in them and tell them to do it. Do what the Lord tells you," she says, "and you won't get into trouble." Pastor Sears nods in agreement.

They like the way of life in the Family Islands. It's slow and peaceful. Hilton, Pastor Sears and Laura Gibson stand tall in their tiny church. Great Exuma and Little Exuma will change with time. The old folk like it just the way it is.

PASTOR C.L. MOSS
ZION BAPTIST CHURCH
FAIR FIELD, CROOKED
ISLAND "I say Lord, the roof of the church is getting bad . . . members dying so fast . . . roof is getting bad. The spirit speak to me. The spirit say 'Go forward'. Then I make a start of getting material for the roof. The Lord will make a way."

Pastor C. L. Moss's voice rings with the sturdy spirit of the people of Fair Field, Crooked Island. The white church is simply designed, with two wood shingle roofs, and a low, white, concrete wall. The church sits on a small hill. Behind the hill the sea sparkles in the brilliant sunshine. Zion Baptist Church's two peaked roofs were built to house the once large congregation. A brass trough runs down from the roof to a cistern to catch the rainwater. Children play on the tiny bell tower outside the church.

The twenty-some members of the congregation are dressed in their Sunday best—flowered dresses, sashes and hats with transparent veils for the women, suits and ties for the men. The temperature is at least ninety degrees in the shade.

The roof of the church is full of holes. Pastor Moss discusses their efforts to raise money. His cousin says they are farmers. They grow what they need to eat. "Since everybody growing the same thing," he says, "you can't sell anything to anybody and Nassau's too far away to ship produce."

MEMBERS OF THE
ZION BAPTIST CHURCH
FAIR FIELD, CROOKED ISLAND

ETHELYN WRING "When Christopher Columbus first found this place, it was called Guanahani, but now it's called San Salvador. He was first landed at a point, Crab Cay we call it, that's where he was first landed. And he left his track there. He put his track and anybody could see it; and there was a monument made. When, he first find this island, he was to get killed the next day, because they was tired; the crew was tired, you know. But the next morning, when he saw the leaves floating, the seaweed, he said, 'leaves floating,' land ahead. And he was very glad."

DELBERT CARTWRIGHT "The Bahamas is what they call the gateway to the western hemisphere. Every ship, every Spanish ship, every ship in the world goes through the Bahama Channel. And everything that sailed would sail by here eventually.

"That's why there's a lot of treasure buried here, that's why you get so many foreign people coming out here looking for treasure. They found quite a few places. I look sometimes, too, but I found out that it's better fun looking for that than finding it . . ."

CHRISTOPHER COLUMBUS MONUMENT
LONG BAY, SAN SALVADOR

CAPTAIN BETHEL, WILLIAMS TOWN, LITTLE EXUMA "The biggest wish I ever had—my granddaddy was on the boat. He had a sailboat and he was on the boat and the wind shift and throw the boom over and he had a hand up on the dinghy; and that boom come cross and take all that skin off and right to the bone. Right down to the bone. And my biggest wish that I wished, I said, 'Lord, I wish that was me instead of him.' I was so sorry for him, you know."

SHIPWRECK, SAN SALVADOR

CHARLES PFLUEGER, MANAGER OF CLUB PEACE & PLENTY   GEORGE TOWN, GREAT EXUMA

"Bonefishing is hunting and fishing in one package, with a lot of relaxing sea around you, and it's a marvelous way to spend the day. The bonefishing probably started around the early fifties here; and Lawrence Lewis who built the Peace & Plenty was one of the people who enjoyed that.

"We've been running a tournament for sixteen years coming up called the Bahamas Bonefish Bonanza. It's in late October every year and we've had a lot of success with it. When we first started fly fishing, it was not done by many of the participants. Now fly fishing probably accounts for . . . oh at least half of the people who come to Exuma to fish. We had a tournament recently where we had more bonefish, it's a release tournament, as all our tournaments are, and we had more bonefish points for fly rods than we did for spinning and I think that's the first time that's happened. We had over 200 fish caught by fly and 150 something caught by spin.

"They're a spooky fish; you drop something in the boat, you talk too loud, you splash an anchor, you make noise and the bonefish will be gone. A cloud can spook them. They think it's an osprey or something. We have ospreys here that go out there, pick up the bonefish and feed on them. We have probably bonefish here in the 14 pound class. The record in the Bahamas is around 20 so you see they don't get too big.

"Bonefishing is a wonderful sport because we don't deplete the supply. Almost all the bonefish are released unless they're hooked in the gills or something and can't be. The local people do eat bonefish but the bonefish means they're bony fish and they're hard to eat. They taste good, but they're bony, but the natives know how to get the meat off the bones.

"The bonefish is a torpedo-type looking fish—silver, almost all silver, with a few dark stripes on him. Sometimes he'll have a dark top side of the fish that let him blend in with grass bottom, or whatever. They're feeding in the mud; one way you find bonefish in deeper water, and I say six to eight feet of water and you're not on the flats, you find the bonefish by looking for the mud, and they call it mudding. And the bonefish will be nosing into the bottom of the water there, in after the crabs and kicking up mud which will discolor the area that they're feeding, so instead of having clear water all around, you'll see a muddy patch.

"It doesn't matter so much the time of day as the tide. The tide is, you need a certain tide on the flats where you can get out and walk it. If it's too deep you can't walk and then they're not there. They're up in the mangrove islands. So when the tide is just right and you have a foot or a foot and a half of water on the flats you can walk the flats and hunt for the bonefish, which is really the way the purists fish for bonefish, with a fly rod, walking the flats on a tide that give them about a foot, eighteen inches of water.

"They're terrific fighters, they're pound for pound probably one of the strongest fish. They don't jump and they're fighting, probably in six inches of water a lot of the times. Very powerful. They take off, it's like tying your line to the back of a car and just having it take off against your drag and it'll really give you a fit. And on a fly rod, it's fabulous, you can be fifteen minutes catching one of the large ones."

PAUL CHRISTIAN PFLUEGER
BONEFISHING, STOCKING ISLAND

CAPTAIN LEVITICUS PATTON, M.V. LADY FRANCIS "In [my] small days, my old man was a captain and I grow up on the sea and it's my life most the time. There are about maybe fifty mail boats in the Bahamas, freight boats, you know. This sleeps thirty-two, with crew and passengers and then some sleep about you know. Sometimes we have about fifty—twenty-five, thirty people sometimes. They sit down until we reach the port, reach where they're going. We go to Rum Cay and then Barraterre and then we go to Farmer's Cay and then to Blackburn, then to Staniel Cay then from there go to Nassau.

"We most exactly bring building stuffs, lumbers, that's important; groceries, peoples—passengers who want to go to the other islands, and different things, food items mostly. This is a mail service we doing now. If the weather too bad we stay to port but if it gets you on the way out we go through it.

"The biggest thing we ever put on was a school bus. Bus was twenty-four feet long. We had something like a chain, chain it down on deck. Keep it even on deck . . . I like the sea life; this is my living and the sea is good. Catch good free fresh air, important things like that."

FELDA MCKENZIE, HANNAH TAYLOR
BARRATERRE, GREAT EXUMA
M.V. LADY FRANCIS

We go out to look for Mr. Romer, or rather 'Dr. Romer', the bush man. He lives in Ramsey, near the new runway at Great Exuma's International Airport. Mr. Romer has gone to a funeral. We drive to the town of Forest. On this hot Sunday, the white church is filled with black people. The array of black clothes, white shirts, bow ties, grey dresses, big hats, black dresses, and white dresses are like a flock of gulls and crows.

The church empties. The funeral procession goes to the cemetery by the sea. The immediate family rides in bright yellow school buses. The minister borrows a woman's large straw hat to keep off the sun. The people surround the freshly dug grave, covered with brightly colored wreaths and flowers. The minister eulogizes Mrs. Marinetha Marie Bodie, eighty-six years old when she died. The crowd of mourners sing church hymns accompanied by gusts of wind and the murmuring sea. Beyond the crowd of mourners, the green and turquoise waters sparkle in the sunshine. Overhead, a grey and white thundercloud masses and towers into the heavens, a fleeting monument to one who had lived by the sea and the wind and the rain.

We meet Joe Romer at the funeral. He takes us to his home. "One thing I like here, if you give out of tea just go in your backyard, get a couple of leaves off different branches and boil your own tea.

"I know how to pick them and put them together. Now for instance, for high blood, I was told that one particular bush that I have been using, they call it Jackmadaw, it's in the sage family, and the Pennywinkler, the red and the white that the people that's in the States they call it Pennywinkler but people here call it Soldier's Cap.

"Now also I was told that the red I believe is for high blood and the white for low blood. So what I do I boil the red along with the Jackmadaw and I makes the medicine according to taste to my liking. If one wants it bitter so I makes it stronger. If one don't want it bitter, I make it milder. Just add water or a little sugar if you want to, as like a tea. For sugar [diabetes] Jackmadaw is also good for the sugar, cause it's a bitter. So I use Jackmadaw for the sugar. What I also do for the sugar, I will take what you call the Sapodilla leaf, soursop leaf, small dilly, dice it up and boil them together and also make a tea from that.

"I changed the name. It was handed down from generation to generation. I call it the Generation Tonic. Well it is, it's from my mother's generation, then it was her parents' generation. So now it's in my generation, so I think it's time at least. The old name, they was calling it 'The Batch', you know. So one time I was trying to get a commercial name for it and I said I'll put Thirteen Plus.

"For the fellas when they want to make them something to sort of give them the strength for pumping and lifting iron and weight. Also they like to use it for the guys in sports—give you a lot of energy for track, whether you're running or whether you're playing the different games of sports like volleyball, baseball, soft or hard ball. And the policemen, they seem to like it.

"What I discovered with the Gamalamie, I had a couple of bites from mosquitoes and they itched me real bad so I just peeled off a piece of the bark of the Gamalamie. I rubbed off a piece of the bark on the skin and pretty soon the itch went away. It's nature itself and everything God made, he made us out of the dirt. "I don't know how we got so far away from the beginning of the creation, but everything came from the dust. We did, the trees, everything. Cause when God created the world he created everything in the world—the trees, the forest, the animals. And he found out he was still lonesome, then he made man. And he found man was lonesome and he made the woman. Now how it got out of hand I can't say, but it's the thing that we all need, each other. And it's the one thing that I have enjoyed here."

JOE ROMER   RAMSEY, GREAT EXUMA

Stella Maris Inn sits at the north end of Long Island, near the airport. Barry went scuba diving to see the feeding of the sharks. Shirlee and I went for a ride. Lost on the roads around Stella Maris, I couldn't find the one highway to the south of the island. I tried driving down a number of dead end roads, but to no avail. Finally, I manoeuvred the car over a pile of dirt obstruction, onto a very wide road, which appeared to be the highway. It was the airport runway.

PHOTOGRAPHS ON PAGES 52–55 BY BARRY BENJAMIN

THIS PAGE Yard of Joe Romer, Ramsey, Great Exuma

OPPOSITE PAGE Spectator at the 1990 Long Island Regatta

PAGE 54–55 Funeral procession, Great Exuma

MANGROVE BUSH, LONG ISLAND

LOVELY ROLLE, WITH VERNON, SHANEISE,
SABRINA, AND JUDITH ROLLE
ROKER'S POINT, GREAT EXUMA

LOVELY ROLLE

"Well I look at one thing, you know. Just what I can do, I do, you know. Just what I can do with my life, well that's in the Lord's hand, the Lord's hand. He holds the future. That's what I believe. I move around and do what I can do and anything else the Lord will take care of that.

"Well, I told my children life is just how you make it. If you make your bed hard, my father just tell us you make your bed hard, you lay hard, if you make it soft, you live soft. All's the thing you have to do, go along in this world, and pray the Lord to guide you. Keep it in his name because there's no other way but the way of the cross, and that what leads you on, cause there's nothing in this world, you know, to look by you. Nothing in this world to look far for.

"Anybody we meet, honor them, have manners; that's the only thing that will take you through the world. If you got manners, if you got manners you're living easier; and if you ain't got no manners you cannot go with everybody.

"You can't live with everyone. Yes, manners take you all through the world. Every place I go so that I can go back. I don't travel much because if I die . . . anywhere I go, I could go back.

"So I think anybody, what my mother tell me I tell my children the same thing. Any old people you meet, got manners with them; manners will take you all through the world. Don't care what you have, ain't have manners. People say we have so and so, but they ain't got no manners."

VERNON ROLLE

"Well, that's the main one I get the teaching from, mother and father. He learn me to go in the world and to work and to make an honest living. He said, 'Boy', he said, 'Listen, by the sweat of your eyebrow you shall eat bread. Don't see anything a person own don't touch it. If you work, you will get something.' And I teach my children the same thing."

SONNY AND EVALENA LLOYD
BARRATERRE, GREAT EXUMA

We drive out to Barraterre on the northern tip of Great Exuma. Sonny Lloyd, blind squeeze box player and bass singer lives in Barraterre and sings with the children in the schools. His great laugh resembles Ray Charles's. Sonny and his sister-in-law Evalena sing gospel hymns and old standard church songs to us. Sonny has a rich bass voice, Evalena a clear soprano. Their voices are full of the black earth that they farm, of the shallow sea that they fish, of the winds from the sea, of the sweat and the toil and the dignity, the kindness and the pride of these people. It is the kind of church singing that could make you weep, or pray, hymns like The Old Rugged Cross, In the Sweet Bye and Bye, Meeting My Friends in the Old Country Church, Come By Here, Amazing Grace.

Sonny is born to make music. His rich bass baritone voice fills the dark room with chords struck from the ark of the church, from the Sunday sermons on sinning and salvation, on damnation, on the body of Christ, on love and on grace whispered, spoken, and shouted like a great hoarse song by the preacher, from the hallelujahs of the congregation, from God.

Sonny and Evalena singing:

There's a place dear to me
where I'm longing to be
With my friends at the old country church
Where with mother we went
and our Sundays were spent
with my friends at the old country church

Precious years of memories
Oh what joy they bring to me
how I long for to be
with my friends at the old country church . . .

Evalena sings the melody in a sweet high soprano voice— her face lit up like sunshine on the mountain top, her eyes looking straight into the face of God. When she talked to us, she was quiet and smiled. She seemed to have little to say, a pleasant chatter. Now as she sings, she is a bird, a rock, mother earth.

Oft my thoughts make me weep
for so many doth sleep
in their graves near the old country church
and sometimes I may rest
with a friend I love best
with my friends at the old country church

Precious years of memories
Oh what joy they bring to me
how I long once more to be
with my friends at the old country church.

Sonny explodes with gentle humor. His face is the coral the islands are made of convoluted, hard and rounded, with quick flashes of expression. He shouts. He laughs. He looks sad. Immediately likeable, Sonny is kind, vivacious and gentle. Experiencing Sonny and Evalena in the remote hamlet on the tip of the big island of Exuma is an unexpected joy, an epiphany.

"See, with me, I sings, you know. I ain't no star, you know. You all ain't looking at me to be no star, but, you know, the most I does I would bass, you know, That's why I been maybe up to the school and while the children would sing their songs I would bass. You see well that's the way I does, what if I go up to the church and they singing songs, well since I'm there they look for me to bass because that's my real talent. I sings bass.

Where the living waters flow
There to dwell in peace forever
and the times of long ago
Friends and loved ones going before me
will be there to welcome me
And we'll sing up there in glory
Sing to all eternity.

"Good, thank you. You have me—arrested. Yeah, you have me arrested. I bass.

Won't you come and go with me
There to live eternally
in that home in glory
We will sing the story
And be glad when . . .

"The accordian, well I been playing it a good while. You know not this one. I had a better one than this. But I was playing it from the time I been I think I was in school. I love music and the school had an accordian, and the headmaster he didn't much mind if I go and fooled with it. You know, I called it fooled with it because, you know, I ain't no pro in no music yet. So I would just go and bother with it and I drilled it. I went out on the road and I would drill it, you know, and so forth. Just like now, I go into the school and I help them with the assembly. Not that I does all but the teacher, she conducted, this was a lady this morning, she conducted the assembly. And I played with them and I bassed with the classes that were there."

"The Simms family came from England. They were early settlers, not loyalists. James Simms started the Simms settlement. I saw what they did in the straw market in Nassau and I tried to do something better. So it was a matter of trial and error. I had no teacher so I tried to design different things, trying to adapt the styles of a leather bag to the straw. We started out with hand machines and we worked on those for quite a number of years. Then we got these foot pedals and they're quite old too. They tell me they're an antique now, the old Singer Sewing Machine.

"The strips are all hand done by the people in their homes and they bring it to me and I buy it by the yard. They each know many patterns. How they ever came by the different patterns I wouldn't know. I did the first handbag.

"The straw comes from a little palm tree called the silver top palm and they cut the leaf before it's blown and dry it in the sun. It's a tan color, you notice the browns, that's the opened leaf. They singe it over a fire and then put it in the sun and it becomes brown. It's equally as strong."

IVY E. SIMMS
SIMMS, LONG ISLAND

"I tell you I don't know why the people on this island are so friendly. 'Cause when I was born my mother be just like that. Everybody is, who don't know each other since he born. I mean, don't be no blood relative, but you still his aunt and uncle and cousin. That's the way we grow, and everybody is friendly really.

"Here is more quiet. City life you have to be going more and you have to be working all the time to live in the city where you have to pay for everything. You got to go and work when you don't feel like it, to meet your end, take care. But here you really don't have to."

> There is beauty all around
> While there's love at home
> Times goes softly, sweetly by
> When there's love at home.
>
> Peace and Plenty here abide
> Smiling sweet on every side
> Time goes softly, sweetly by
> When there's love at home.
>
> Love at home
> Love at home
> Time goes softly, sweetly by
> When there's love at home.
>
> Peace and plenty here abide
> Smiling sweet on every side
> Time goes sweetly, softly by
> When there's love at home.

QUOTE AND SONG SUNG: ETHELYN WRING "We have to walk. The settlement they call Cockburn Town, twelve miles. We walk twelve miles. That was terrible. Didn't have no transportation you know. We have to walk. To go to church sometimes we'd go to church in the next settlement we'd start about three o'clock in the morning and we'd walk and then we get to church, get dressed and go to church. And come back the same way. It was tough, but it was better for us.

"We go in the field, we have to work, weed the bush, weed the bush, come back again. Go next morning and then plant corn, plant peas. You go and weed the crop. Everything weeding. The corn, we stick some of it in a drum and have a corn mill, and have to grind it. Corn mill that we turn with the hand. Then we cook. We used to go pond, the big pond, big bundle of clothes we carry in the pond and wash all day. Hang them out, they white as snow. Then we go in the bushes and get something we call starch. We come home, clean out the starch, have a great tray make nice starch, starch our clothes, and then iron it nice and stiff. Wood, you have to go in the bushes and get wood, put on our head bring biggest bundle of wood home. You cook on the fire, you know. You have pots, and cook in the fire."

ELOISE LIGHTFOOT WITH JERRETTE
UNITED ESTATES, SAN SALVADOR

CHILDREN FROM MT. THOMPSON PRIMARY SCHOOL
GREAT EXUMA

PASTOR REX MAJORS SPEAKING ABOUT HIS FATHER, NGM MAJORS

". . . he struggled with grades, I remember that. Because he knew no child could achieve, necessarily, as much as another when that other is more blessed with ability and talent. But yet each could achieve. And that's why the agriculture thing to him was important . . . You know, if you're a great farmer, you're a great man. You don't have to be just someone working for that wage kind of thing . . . You use what you have; you make the most of what's around you. You don't create false worlds or false images or false visions or false dreams.

". . . so he helped the people, for instance, in this community. You notice it's a farming community. One of his abiding results is the application of using whatever ground you have—sow something, plant something. So a lot of that stuff that you see now came out of that same feeling, because . . . he taught every child how to bud a tree, for instance. All the boys learned how to bud. Every single boy had to do that. You had to do it.

"So it was his application to life—to the life you now live, not just the life that may be tomorrow. It wasn't a dream world.

"I'm committed to the reality that fantasy is destruction. That reality is life. Dreams that are impossible are a waste of time. They remain bubbles.

"The tamarind tree in the school yard—it's one of the oldest, lasting pieces that remain through the years. It fell down in a storm and it grew parallel with the ground for awhile and created a natural bench and because of the shade it became a classroom. Each class, in turn, used that tamarind tree for some lesson, and, of course, from the tamarind tree came the almighty switch as well, which really tanned the bottom of many of us, left us red, and so it's a part of us."

"What's the use of being worth something when nobody knows but you. That's why I brag sometimes, you know."

NGM MAJORS
DEADMAN'S CAY, LONG ISLAND

"From the very beginning the first people that was here was the Arawak Indians. During the days of piracy when the pirates was all through the Bahama Islands, the Indians was here. When the early settlers came I'd say in the late 1500's, we had over twelve thousand Arawak on this island. The settlers came here mainly from England, a few from Sweden. But the Indians were here before Columbus came around 1492.

"The early settlers acquired huge tracts of land from the queen reigning at that particular time. They paid what you call preference on the spot, but they paid it in installments until they paid up the amount and then they got the title for it. They brought slaves here when they came here to do the labor for them, that's what built these huge plantations that they had. They was trading them up and down through the Caribbean and other islands.

"After they got these plantations set up, the main industry then that they had was cotton, cotton and cattle too. Then other things that went along with it. They didn't do so well on the cotton. Some of the soil wasn't suitable for cotton and the island being so narrow, it got dashed from the heavy northeasterners and the fierce winds that brought the salt spray across the land. And then after that they had this bug that came in and got into the cotton.

"The main source of living then was off of stock farming, you know, cattle, cows, and sheep and hog and goats and chickens. What really amazes me is how they survived because they were the first people here, but they didn't have much contact with the outside world.

"I guess boats came now and again, that's why they built these huge plantations on the highest hills they could find, so they could all look both sides of the island to see when the boats came in. I guess mainly they survived off the land. After the cotton industry, next came the pineapple industry.

"Boats that came here from Baltimore used to come up by Clarence Town, buy the pineapples and take them to the United States to sell so they did pretty good off the pineapples while they lasted. The stinging ant came and got into the heart of the pineapple and they didn't have anything to kill them with so they just threw them out. And then they started to grow pineapples in other parts of the world which was much closer to the United States than here."

DELBERT CARTWRIGHT
GRAYS, LONG ISLAND

KEVIN BROWN, ANTOINE FERGUSON
FOREST, GREAT EXUMA

ROSALEE, GEORGIA AND WILLIE WRIGHT
ANNASTRACK, GREAT EXUMA

TRACEY STILES, WILLIAMS TOWN, LITTLE EXUMA "They used to ship salt from here to North Carolina and various places. The ship, the slaver, used to have 160 slaves and they used to harvest the salt, 16,000 bushels here. They used to ship it to the United States and foreign countries. And they usually make the salt the way they wanted to make it. Make it in the ponds, the islanders just cut up, whenever they want to make the salt they just drain the pond and put in the brine and make the salt and just harvest that amount of salt. Dry out the ponds and then put the brine in it and let it dry and it forms salt. And they had the outlet for it. The ships used to come in and take the salt to foreign countries.

"Now that monument you see down there that was the landmark for the ships when they come in here; they come in straight and they would know that's the place where they could come in for the salt.

"You know the old airport where you see the iron ramp out there? [author's note: about fifteen miles away] I used to knock off four o'clock on Saturday and walk home with probably about thirty pound rice on my shoulder and come home and got to be to work Sunday morning. Leave George Town four o'clock, come up and check mother out and then pick me up some clean clothes and six, seven o'clock on Sunday you got to be back to work. And if you hadn't be back to work you probably may lose your job. There was times it was raining and you just got to go through the rain. If not, you don't be back to work and the man want you he just lay you off for a week. Punish you for that.

"Go down to work and you don't reach on time he tell you to go home for a week. You got to walk back up here and if you wanted the job during the week, you got to go back there. And a lot of folks, you could only afford to wear shoes when you were going to church. Who had one, who had a pair of shoes only wear when you're going to church. But wearing shoes during the week, you couldn't afford it. Yeah, I've been wearing shoes from the day I could afford to buy one I wear shoes. Yeah, I seen a lot of tough days."

ALVERNA MAJOR SIMMS, LONG ISLAND

ARRIE PERCENTIE, FARMER'S CAY

"Farmer's Cay has grown and those persons has had children and those children has had children. This land, no one here can sell it or buy it. But it's ours and our children's children and it'll be throughout the generations. Well that attracted a lot of us, and that sort of dismay a lot of us so I guess the majority is . . . I guess that's why Farmer's Cay is scanty. Everyone don't agree with that kind of makeup. But that's what we have to live with.

"We make our living here by small curriculas. Marine, like conch and fish, a little detail work here, a little detail work there. That was our school building up there. All of my days in the school was right in the church building. The government sort of put up a school building there. My little brother is going to benefit from that. And that's basically what Farmer's Cay is about. We are an inhabitant right now of about thirty to forty-five. When all that ought to be represented by the houses built here was here we would be about sixty. But as it is now about thirty to forty-five."

REBECCA HUNT
UNITED ESTATES, SAN SALVADOR

GERALD AND ELKIN FLOWERS
FARMER'S HILL, GREAT EXUMA